RABINDRANATH TAGORE

Final Poems

RABINDRANATH TAGORE

Final Poems

SELECTED AND TRANSLATED

FROM THE BENGALI BY

WENDY BARKER AND

SARANINDRANATH TAGORE

George Braziller

NEW YORK

The publisher and translators extend their thanks to
Visva-Bharati University for permission to publish these translations.

For information, please address the publisher:
George Braziller, Inc.
171 Madison Avenue
New York, New York 10016

Library of Congress Cataloging-in-Publication Data
Tagore, Rabindranath, 1861–1941.
Rabindranath Tagore : final poems / selected and translated
from the Bengali by Wendy Barker and Saranindranath Tagore.
p. cm.
Includes bibliographical references.
ISBN 0-8076-1488-2
1. Tagore, Rabindranath, 1861–1941—Translations into English.
I. Barker, Wendy. II. Tagore, Saranindranath. III. Title.
PK1722.A2 B37 2001
891.4′414—dc21 2001037897

FRONTISPIECE: Rabindranath Tagore, ca. 1940.
From the archives of Rabindra Bhavan, Shantiniketan.

Design by Neko Buildings

Printed and bound in the United States of America

FIRST EDITION

ACKNOWLEDGMENTS

We are grateful to the editors of the following journals, in which several of these translations originally appeared, some in slightly different versions:

The Hollins Critic: Sickbed 9 and *Recovery* 24
International Poetry Review: Sickbed 23 and *Recovery* 25
The Kenyon Review and *Stand Magazine: Sickbed* 5 and 7,
    Recovery 30, *On My Birthday* 8, and *Last Poems* 2 and 4
The Literary Review:An International Quarterly: Recovery 9
Manoa:A Pacific Journal of International Writing: Sickbed 17,
    26, and 35, *Recovery* 6, and *Last Poems* 10 and 14
Michigan Quarterly Review: Sickbed 27 and *Recovery* 22
    and 31
the new renaissance: Sickbed 39 and *Recovery* 4
Nimrod: International Journal of Prose and Poetry: Recovery 3
Partisan Review: On My Birthday 28

We are deeply indebted to the work of Krishna Dutta and Andrew Robinson, William Radice, Ketaki Kushari Dyson, Shyamasree Devi, and P. Lal.

Grateful acknowledgment is also due Visva-Bharati University for permission to publish these translations; in particular we wish to thank Swapan Majumdar and Kalyan Moitra of Visva-Bharati for their support of our work. The insightful comments of the university reviewer helped with our revisions.

We also extend our gratitude to the University of Texas at San Antonio, for research grants that gave us time to work; to the National University of Singapore; to Alicia Ostriker and Sudeep Sen, for helpful reactions in the early stages of our translations; and to Amritjit Singh, for generous suggestions on matters often extending beyond linguistics. Our editors at George Braziller have been ideal; we are particularly grateful to Mary Taveras for intelligent care.

Most of all, we are grateful to our families for help that came in many versions: Saranindranath's parents, Sumitendranath and Shyamasree Tagore; his wife, Mita Tagore; and Wendy's companion, Steven G. Kellman, have supported us in more ways than we can adequately acknowledge here. Saranindranath's sons, Shayonendranath and Shlokendranath, and Wendy's son, David, have provided encouragement in ways we trust they will come to understand.

CONTENTS

PREFACE

I first came across the poems of Rabindranath Tagore as a high-school student. The selections I read from the Nobel Prize winner's work were taken primarily from *Gitanjali* and *Fireflies* and were translated by the poet. I was "changed utterly," to use William Butler Yeats's phrase, by my reading of Tagore—I had found, as Emily Dickinson put it, "Another way—to see."

Throughout the years that followed and through dozens of moves, the thick turquoise anthology that contained Tagore's poems kept its place on an easily accessible bookshelf. Once in a while I would flip through and find Tagore again:

> In the mountain, stillness surges up
> to explore its own height;
> in the lake, movement stands still
> to contemplate its own depth.[1]

Such moments of stillness were (and are) hard to come by. It was during a period of little stillness and of much doubt that a living link to Rabindranath Tagore walked into my office and made me an offer I could not refuse: that we collaborate on a translation of the poems Tagore wrote during the last year of his life.

Saranindranath Tagore and I had been friendly colleagues for several years by the fall of 1993. Bappa, as everyone calls him, was one of our philosophers at the University of Texas at San Antonio, and during his first year at our university I had asked him if by any chance he was connected to the poet Tagore. I am not sure which of us was more delighted: Bappa, that I knew of his great-grandfather's[2] illustrious uncle, that I was familiar with his ancestor's poems, and that I even knew his first name (although I mispronounced it, saying Rab-in-DRA-nuth rather than Rab-IN-druh-nath); or I, that I had refound Tagore.

I had been translating with another colleague from the Italian of Eugenio Montale and had found the process a compelling challenge. And I had traveled in Italy. While I was not fluent in Italian, still, I was quick with a dictionary and could get what I needed from a *trattoria* or a *farmacia*. Translating Tagore would be an entirely different challenge. Although over the years since first discovering the poems of Tagore, I had been an avid but infrequent reader of Asian poetry and philosophy, I had never been to India. Unable to decipher a single squiggle of the Bengali editions Bappa brought for us to work from, I did not even know the difference between Hindi and Bengali.

What I did not know then was that my linguistic ignorance was somewhat of an advantage. I had no idea what our destination was—or even where we would begin. When Bappa arrived at my house for our translating sessions, I entered an open space, an "unknown region," to quote Walt Whitman. The journey of our translating was an "Open Road"; of necessity, I became "loos'd of limits and imaginary lines."

The poems we have translated are taken from the four collections Rabindranath Tagore wrote during the last year of his life, between May 1940 and July 1941: *Rogsajyāy,* or *Sickbed; Ārogya,* or *Recovery; Janmandine,* or *On My Birthday;* and *Sheś Lekhā,* or *Last Poems* (one poem, *On My Birthday 24,* was written earlier, on 25 February 1939). Close to death, recovering only briefly and partially, Tagore unblinkingly faced his own extinction. These are poems written by a man in extreme pain, who is, even on "good days," excruciatingly weak. The poems express terror, awe, anger, grief, as well as acceptance, wonder, exhilaration, and even joy at the imminent prospect of setting out for the ultimate "unknown regions."

The group of poems from the shortest of the volumes, *Sheś Lekhā,* had been translated into English and published in India in 1972 by Shyamasree Devi and P. Lal, and a few poems from the four collections have been translated and published separately. But until now no sustained effort has been made to bring out a selection from this body of poetry, which signals a marked departure from everything else Tagore wrote during his immensely productive life. Still present in these poems are Tagore's musical devices, his delicious play with the Bengali language. But the language here is stripped, austere, direct, and, as Ezra Pound might have said, close to the bone. Tagore's language is so compact it is almost as if the poet were going beyond words, as if language no longer sufficed, and yet, of course, the language radiates meaning.

Bappa and I would begin with his initial reading aloud of a poem in Bengali while I listened to the entirely unfamiliar sounds, the rushes of rhythms so different from English, the intonations (which gradually became, of course, less and less strange). I listened to the music of the poem. Then, line by line, word by word, Bappa gave me equivalents in English. Sometimes we had a column of a dozen English possibilities for one word, none of them acceptable. We spent hours flipping through dictionaries, his and mine.

But early on we realized that we had no chance of recreating the musical and linguistic complexities of Tagore's fluid and nuanced Bengali. Instead, we decided to strive to create the mood and tone of a poem and to use ordinary American colloquial diction, since these poems, unlike much of the poet's earlier work, are informal, compact, direct, and, for the most part, written in free verse. They often draw upon his experiences in the rural areas of Bengal, at his beloved Shantiniketan, or on the River Padma (Bengalis pronounce it "Pohddah"), from the days he supervised villagers and farming people on his family's outlying estates. They give no hint of the vast public career behind the eighty-year-old man, "myriad minded," as his biographers Krishna Dutta and Andrew Robinson describe him, and as much an international celebrity and influence as his fellow countryman Mohandas Gandhi (whom Tagore endowed with the epithet "Mahatma").

In India today, the name Rabindranath Tagore is as ubiquitous as turmeric and is revered by literati and laity alike. Reverence for "Rabi" or "Gurudev" has, in fact, taken such extreme forms that it is even parodied in Vikram Seth's lush novel of Indian family life, *A Suitable Boy,* in which the voluble Mrs. Chatterji effuses over rosy girlhood memories of "her master, the waterer of the garden of the culture of Bengal."[3] Yet even the hip young urban sophisticates who scorn Mrs. Chatterji's nostalgic adoration of the "master" are themselves flowers and fruit of the cultural garden nurtured by Tagore, which is perhaps why some young Bengali writers today try to think about Tagore as little as possible. As Dante is to Italy, Tagore is to India, and the prospect of following such a dazzling career is a daunting one.

Tagore's oeuvre—the result of an intensely creative life extending beyond six decades—includes twenty-eight large volumes of poems, dramas, operas, short stories, novels, essays, and diaries. He completed about two thousand drawings and paintings and wrote more than twenty-five hundred songs. And although his songs are the works best known and most loved by Bengalis, other works are not only still widely read and studied but also frequently performed. It is not an overstatement to say that throughout South Asia and even East Asia, the name Tagore is a household word.

Although Tagore dedicated much of his life to causes other than literary ones, especially to education, instigating pedagogical reforms throughout India, and although his works of prose writings are voluminous, he is best known, not only in Bengal but also around the globe, as a poet. And of course his 1913 Nobel Prize, largely due to the reception of his translated collection of poems *Gitanjali,* enthusiastically touted by Yeats, established Tagore's reputation in the West. But oddly, whereas his poems as well as novels and short stories are so widely translated and available in European and Latin American countries that one can find editions of Tagore's works in paperback racks in train stations in Milan and Buenos Aires, even his poetry is little known in the United States.

Americans' lack of familiarity with one of the twentieth century's great poets may be due to the difficulties of translating his poems into English. Pragmatic Anglo-Saxon culture has been less amenable to the kinds of abstractions that could more easily find a home in the language of Cervantes. And if, as George Steiner has suggested, to "translate is to descend beneath the exterior disparities of two languages in order to bring into vital play their analogous and, at the final depths, common principles of being,"[4] translating Tagore's Bengali into accessible American English necessitates diving to such underwater depths that one must be careful not to get "the bends."

The English language simply has no equivalents for many concepts basic to Indian thought. Take, for example, the word *māyā*. Usually, *māyā* is translated as "illusion," a word that throughout its history has suggested deceit, or error, something unreal. (*Illusion* comes originally from the Latin *inludere,* "to mock.") But the Hindu concept of maya, while referring to appearances that are indeed illusionary in that they are perceived at the empirical or sensory level, also suggests the undifferentiated spiritual reality that has created the illusion in the first place. One word suggests both the veil of the illusion and the great play of spheres beyond it. My third edition of *The American Heritage Dictionary* defines *maya* as:

1. The power of a god or demon to transform a concept into an element of the sensible world. 2. The transitory, manifold appearance of the sensible world, which obscures the undifferentiated spiritual reality from which it originates; the illusory appearance of the sensible world.[5]

But even this careful definition does not provide the nuances of the twenty-line explanation found in *The Encyclopedia of Eastern Philosophy and Religion,* which discusses the Hindu concept of maya (the Buddhist and Zen concepts require an additional twenty lines) as "ignorance or cosmic illusion" that veils our vision, separating us from *Brahman,* "so that we see only the diversity of the universe rather than the one reality." (The one reality is *Brahman,* the "eternal, imperishable Absolute," a concept with no equivalent in dualistic religious thought. *Brahman* is absolute being, absolute consciousness, absolute bliss, a state of pure transcendence that cannot be grasped by thought or speech.)[6] And this definition is simple and brief in comparison with the far more specific explanation in John Grimes's *Concise Dictionary of Indian Philosophy.*

Perhaps our biggest stumbling block was what to do with Bengali words such as these, words meaning "faith," "consciousness," and "being," which are as central to Indian philosophical thought as rice is to dinner. Ever since Ezra Pound said, "Go in fear of abstractions," and perhaps ever since World War I, with Ernest Hemingway's admonition in *A Farewell to Arms* that words like *honor* and *glory* had become "obscene," American poetry has eschewed abstractions, particularly those having to do with spiritual concepts. In a recent letter, poet and translator Stanley Burnshaw confessed (or affirmed), "I am constitutionally unable to read a good deal of writing that is full of such words as 'faith, Truth,' and other such abstractions in which the literature of some of the 'Eastern' writers and thinkers abounds. My limitation, I know. Alas, alas!"[7] And words like *faith* and *truth* have, of course, been overused to the point that they have become illusionary themselves, meaningless. We have tried to use fresh language in English, cognizant always of the fact that even if Tagore is using a common abstract concept in Bengali, his language is musical, playful, resonant, and layered. But at times we have simply used a word like *faith,* at our wits' end to find English-language alternatives that would be true enough to Tagore's Bengali. At other times we decided simply to use the Bengali word. In *Recovery* 9, we just say *maya*—only two syllables, and we are assuming that most Anglophone readers have a strong sense of what the word implies. Our overall policy, however, was to find an English-language equivalent and keep the use of Bengali words to a minimum.

The differences between languages and cultures are found even in superficial matters such as clothing. In *Recovery* 3, for instance, the poet uses the word *ghomtā,* referring to the part of the sari that can be pulled up over the head of the wearer. There is no English word for this part of the garment. The word *sari* would convey a specific visual image to most readers in the United States (it is even defined in my *American Heritage Dictionary*), but the vividness of this section of the poem depends upon the reader's knowledge that the village girls' heads are covered. There is a haunting, although innocent and charming, quality about the girls walking the path, their faces not visible while their whispers are audible. Here, we gave up economy and lyricism and added words, trying to evoke the image's clarity. Our compromise reads:

> Sun-dazzled urns balanced on their waists, village girls'
> whispers under saris pulled over their heads
> echo the path, winding. . . .

At least with clothes we can create a clear image, even if we arrive at a wooden phrase like this one. With anything sensory we are on far firmer ground than we are with philosophy.

But none of these challenges has been as frustrating (and, strangely, as exhilarating) as dealing with Bengali words that convey not only multiple, but even contradictory meanings. English is, of course, not entirely devoid of such words; one thinks of *sanction,* for instance, which can mean either "to approve" or "to condemn." But Bengali is rich with words that contain their own opposites, that are themselves paradoxes. In *Recovery* 24, for example, Tagore uses the Bengali word *marjādā*. In these three syllables Tagore conveys notions of prestige, honor, tradition, esteem, and fame, as well as a sense of boundaries or limits. Following usual Anglophone associational patterns, a native English speaker would probably assume that prestige and fame could enable one to move past limits, to break beyond boundaries, but in the Bengali, this word suggests that prestige and honor, by their very nature, necessitate boundaries, limits. To make matters more difficult, Tagore is using the word to mean *without* these qualities. We are not especially proud of our compromise: we decided on "fameless, limitless." We comfort ourselves by saying that at least our phrase is reasonably compact and informal. But our English pales beside the poet's Bengali.

Overall, we have tried to keep as close to Tagore's Bengali as possible. To that end, we have worked through each poem word by word; often, in order to keep the tone of the poem, or its ambiguities, we have retained Tagore's syntactical order, even though the phrasing would be rearranged in English. Because so much of Tagore's poetic brilliance depends upon his playfulness and ambiguity, we did everything possible to convey these qualities. In a few instances, we rearranged two or three lines (as in *Recovery* 9, where we reversed lines eleven and twelve), but only if the sense of the poem would be lost if we kept the original order. Occasionally we have changed a line break if the rhythm in English became awkward by keeping Tagore's lineation. In most cases we have kept very short lines that in English might seem rather weak, such as "I know" in *Sickbed* 26, where the line conveys an emphasis that would be lost if these two words were joined to a line above or below. We have sometimes omitted modifiers, but only when we felt that the English-language adjective weakened an otherwise strong image. One particular modifying word or phrase Tagore uses often in these poems translates in English to "suddenly," or "in a flash." In some instances, it seemed that an effect of greater suddenness would be created if we left out the modifier, so the line itself comes "in a flash," as in *Sickbed* 7, where we have changed line three from the closer translation, "when suddenly I see" to, simply, "when I see."

One characteristic of Tagore's Bengali that we had difficulty conveying is the use of compound nouns, which can have a powerful effect similar to that of the Norse, Icelandic, and Anglo-Saxon kenning (as in "whale-road" for "ocean"). These can take the form in the poet's original language of two nouns joined to form one (not unlike the German practice), or of two or three nouns used side by side (at times these are hyphenated) with no preposition or indicator of possession. In English, our tendency would be to turn one of these nouns into a modifier, an adjective, or a prepositional phrase (to use the example of "whale-road," we would normally tend to say "the whales' road" or "the road of whales"). In *Recovery* 31, we managed a fairly direct translation: "sunset-glaze" is close to the original. But all too often we found that for clarity, or for purposes of rhythm or internal rhyme, we needed to make the syntax of our phrasing more typical of English usage. In *Recovery* 3, we omitted "self" from "self-form," so that our phrase reads simply: "the form of the gods." In *Recovery* 14, we changed "self-surrender" to "utter surrender." In *Sickbed* 23 we decided not to use the more literal "unvisioned creation-streams," and opted instead for "unseen, untold streams—all creation." But always our fear has been that we would, by too much tinkering, further obscure Tagore's brilliant use of Bengali. Even Yeats, in his enthusiasm for Tagore's early work, made typescript changes that ignored the possibilities these compound nouns can create, as when he changed the phrase "trophy garlands" to "trophies and garlands" in *Gitanjali* 4.[8]

William Butler Yeats was, of course, one of Rabindranath Tagore's first poetic champions in the West. He comments in his introduction to the 1913 edition of *Gitanjali*: "I have carried the manuscript of these translations about with me for days, reading it in railway trains, or on the top of omnibuses and in restaurants, and I have often had to close it lest some stranger would see how much it moved me."[9] His enthusiasm was infectious. He introduced the visiting Bengali to Ezra Pound, who said Tagore made him "feel like a painted pict with a stone war-club."[10] About *Gitanjali,* Pound said he found in the poems "a sort of ultimate common sense, a reminder of one thing and of forty things of which we are over likely to lose sight in the confusion of our Western life, in the racket of our cities, in the jabber of manufactured literature, in the vortex of advertisement."[11] Other early enthusiasts influenced by Tagore include Wilfred Owen, T. Sturge Moore, Juan Ramón Jiménez, Leonard Woolf, Anna Akhmatova, Hart Crane, and Robert Frost. In 1912, editor Harriet Monroe accepted several of Tagore's poems for her Chicago-based *Poetry* magazine, convinced by Pound's letter that the Bengali's verses would "be the sensation of the winter."[12] During his visits to the United States in 1912–13 and again in 1916–17, Tagore indeed became a sensation, a visible and controversial figure touring the country, lecturing.

But even those most enthusiastic about Tagore were not without ambivalence. It was only after she finished translating Tagore in the 1960s that Anna Akhmatova asserted, "He's a great poet"; while working on the poems, she continually and caustically criticized them.[13] William Ralph Inge, dean of St. Paul's Cathedral, noted in his diary, after hearing a lecture by Tagore, "It was a beautiful exposition of pure mystical doctrine, but I could not help feeling that there was no concrete filling."[14] Tagore's biographers Krishna Dutta and Andrew Robinson describe George Bernard Shaw as highly skeptical, regarding Tagore with "a mixture of respect and ridicule," jokingly referring to him as "Old Bluebeard" and naming a character in a play "Stupendranath Begorr." Bertrand Russell was even more derisive in characterizing one of Tagore's lectures as "unmitigated rubbish."[15] And although Tagore was described in the *New York Times* as "the greatest secular figure in the world" during his tour of the United States in 1916 and 1917, he also met with criticism and even scorn. The *Nation*'s Paul Elmer More castigated the Bengali celebrity for disseminating "spiritual pap," growling that he himself would find consolation "from philosophers who at least have the advantage of being virile."[16]

Such strong mixed Western reactions to Tagore may also explain at least partly why the poet's work was virtually ignored for most of the twentieth century in the practical-minded United States. Even the excitement over his American visits fueled suspicion about the bearded "exotic," solidifying many Western stereotypical notions of Tagore as an insubstantial mystic. And, as Tagore's early biographer Edward Thompson lamented, whereas the verses of *Gitanjali*—the collection that first attracted attention from Yeats, Pound, and others of the Western literary world—have little in common with the short stories, essays, novels, and plays of Tagore, nevertheless these little poems were what fixed Tagore's image in the West as an ineffectual dreamer.[17] Of course, such misconceptions developed primarily because of stereotypical attitudes based on Westerners' ignorance of the depth and diversity of Indian culture, as well as the variety of Tagore's accomplishments. Few Americans know that Tagore was a major education reformer in his native country, developing a school at Shantiniketan that grew into Visva-Bharati University and working to reform education throughout the country. He emphasized the importance of teaching not only in English but especially in indigenous languages. He also played an active role in the Swadeshi movement, working devotedly (although his methods differed from Gandhi's) for Indian independence. Widely read in Western literature and history, he was heavily criticized in his own country for being too Western.

"The cultural gap between East and West," the filmmaker

Satyajit Ray said about Western attitudes to Indian cinema in 1963, "is too wide for a handful of films to reduce it."[18] Certainly Ray did his best to bring Tagore to the public, basing many of his films on stories by his elder countryman, several of which are available in the United States. And by India's fiftieth anniversary of independence in 1997, the cultural gap had narrowed considerably. Not only are writers like Salman Rushdie and Anita Desai almost household names, at least among serious readers of contemporary fiction, but an entirely new generation of Indian writers—including Vikram Seth, Shashi Tharoor, Amitav Ghosh, Arundhati Roy, and Desai's daughter, Kiran Desai—is also being acclaimed and embraced far beyond India's borders. In the spring of 1997, the British journal *Granta* devoted an entire issue to India's writers, and that same year, one of the most enduring and popular magazines of the United States, *National Geographic,* devoted much of its May issue to Indian culture.

Readers in the United States are now far less ignorant about Indian literature and culture—in fact, since the anniversary of independence in 1997, India has been a trendy topic. This may at least partially be due to the impact of the large numbers of recent Indian émigrés, who are doing much to dispel the fog of ignorance about India that blanketed the United States for decades.[19] Living as we do in what some have called the Diasporic Age, we need available English translations of Tagore's works more than ever. Tagore's prose has, of course, already appeared in various places and forms in English translation. In 1996, for example, Tagore's biographers Dutta and Robinson brought out an English translation of his play *The Post Office;* in 1997, they published an anthology of Tagore's writings, which includes letters, essays, and short stories, as well as twenty-one poems. But although Dutta and Robinson, William Radice, Ketaki Kushari Dyson, and Amiya Chakravarty, among others (including Tagore himself), have translated a number of Tagore's earlier poems into English, this is the first collection, in English, of the poems written during the poet's final year.

One of the facts Rabindranath Tagore learned and delighted in as a child was that, while the Sun appeared to be small to the human eye, it was actually thousands of times bigger than Earth. Since *rabi* in Bengali means "sun," this bit of information appealed to the boy even more.[20] These final poems, seemingly very small, even in their sparseness, express much of the depth and range of the man who was Rabindranath Tagore. And that man was, first and foremost, as he himself insisted, primarily a poet.

Just before Tagore's death in the summer of 1941, he was moved from the trees and open air of Shantiniketan back to the noise and clamor of Calcutta. The crowd surrounding his funeral procession was so dense that it was impossible for his son to press through the chaos to light his father's funeral pyre. On 2 January 1941, in the quiet of Shantiniketan, about seven months before he died, Tagore had written:

> Let the time to leave
> be quiet, still. Let no pompous memorials
> build the hypnosis of grieving.

Let the lines of trees by the departure door
bestow the tranquil chanting of earth
on quiet heaps of leaves.
Let night's soundless blessing slowly descend,
iridescent offerings of the seven stars.[21]

The last works of many great artists are marked by a transcendence and sublimity uncharacteristic of earlier creations—one thinks of William Shakespeare's *The Tempest,* of Beethoven's late string quartets, and of Claude Monet's *Water Lilies,* which, like these last poems of Tagore, dissolve boundaries. Here, in his final poems, it is as if the poet were poised between two states of being, at times speaking to us from another place, a place beyond "this mortal coil." He seems to use a language beyond language—and our English words cannot help but fall short.

—WENDY BARKER

Notes

1. Rabindranath Tagore, *Fireflies,* trans. Rabindranath Tagore (New York: The Macmillan Company, 1944), p. 25.

2. The painter Abanindranath Tagore is widely recognized as the father of modern Indian art.

3. Vikram Seth, *A Suitable Boy* (New York: HarperCollins, 1993), p. 1202.

4. George Steiner, *After Babel: Aspects of Language and Translation* (London, Oxford, and New York: Oxford University Press, 1975), p. 73.

5. *The American Heritage Dictionary of the American Language,* 4th ed., s.v. "maya."

6. Stephan Schuhmacher, Gert Woerner, et al., eds., *The En-*

cyclopedia of Eastern Philosophy and Religion (Boston: Shambala Publications, Inc., 1989), pp. 223–24.

7. Stanley Burnshaw to Wendy Barker, personal letter, 12 July 2000.

8. Typescript of William Butler Yeats's manuscript corrections of Gitanjali, the Berg Collection, New York Public Library.

9. Rabindranath Tagore, Gitanjali: A Collection of Indian Songs, trans. Rabindranath Tagore (1913; reprint, New York: Macmillan Publishing Company, 1971), p. 12.

10. Rabindranath Tagore: An Anthology, ed. Krishna Dutta and Andrew Robinson (New York: St. Martin's Press, 1997), p. 2.

11. Ibid., p. 2.

12. Krishna Dutta and Andrew Robinson, Rabindranath Tagore: The Myriad-Minded Man (New York: St. Martin's Press, 1995), p. 171.

13. Ibid., p. 5.

14. Ibid., p. 175.

15. Ibid., p. 176.

16. Paul Elmer More, "Rabindranath Tagore," The Nation, 30 November 1916, pp. 506–7.

17. E. P. Thompson, Alien Homage: Edward Thompson and Rabindranath Tagore (New Delhi: Oxford University Press, 1993), p. 49.

18. Satyajit Ray, Our Films Their Films (Bombay: Orient Longman, 1976), p. 161.

19. U.S. Census figures show that new immigration laws in 1965 resulted in 164,134 legal immigrants arriving in the United States from India between 1971 and 1980; 261,841 arrived between 1981 and 1990. Between 1970 and 1998, 722,000 legal immigrants from India entered the United States.

20. Dutta and Robinson, Myriad-Minded Man, p. 57.

21. From Recovery 31, translation by Wendy Barker and Saranindranath Tagore.

INTRODUCTION

I

One of the last letters that Rabindranath Tagore wrote before his death at the age of eighty on 7 August 1941 was a condolence letter:

> Shantiniketan, [West Bengal, India]
> 10 July, 1941
>
> Dear Child
>
> I am deeply grieved to learn of the tragedy that has overtaken your life. I will not insult your sorrow by any cheap consolation. We are all tragically helpless before Fate, since we cannot protect the happiness of those we care for. We can only sympathise. You have to bear the weight of your sorrow till your own strength and the mercy of time help you to rise over it.
>
> Yours sincerely
> Rabindranath Tagore[1]

There is nothing extraordinary about this letter. It contains a few words of comfort written to a woman who had recently lost someone she loved. Yet this simple act of condolence is of a piece with some of the great poetic evocations of death in world literature. Between 1940 and 1941, after partially recovering from a life-threatening illness, Rabindranath wrote, among other works, about a hundred poems shaped by a consciousness approaching death. Too weak to hold a pen, he dictated the last of these poems to his secretary hours before a final surgery from which he never recovered.

You hold in your hands a selection of these poems. Let me say a few words about the poet; I will then return to the poems.

Though the poet is known around the world as Tagore, I will call him Rabindranath (the name means "lord of the sun"), following the Bengali custom of addressing poets by their first names.

II

Rabindranath Tagore (1861–1941) is one of the greatest cultural figures of modern India. He was born into a Calcutta family that was at the forefront of the political and social renaissance that shaped the life of the city in the nineteenth century. Rabindranath's grandfather, Dwarkanath Tagore, was a leading Indian entrepreneur with diversified business interests. He tirelessly sought to support his friend Rammohan Ray in his numerous reform efforts such as the banning of the institution of widow immolation. Rabindranath's father, Debendranath, is regarded as one of the great architects of the new Hinduism and is a towering figure in the history of Indian religious thought. Rabindranath's older brother, Jyotirindranath, was a composer, a dramatist, and a translator of literature from European languages.

His sister, Swarnakumari Devi, was a novelist of great originality. His nephews, Abanindranath and Gaganedranath, are two great figures in the history of modern Indian art.

Born into such an illustrious family, Rabindranath's life is studded with achievements that are astonishing in their breadth and scale. As a writer, he was a poet, a novelist, a short-story writer, an essayist on a rich diversity of topics, a dramatist who produced and acted in his own plays, and a lifelong writer of magnificent letters. He was also a composer of almost two thousand songs called *Rabindrasangīt* that created an entirely new style within Indian musical traditions. Rabindranath, in fact, is the only composer in the world whose songs stand today as the national anthem of two independent nations: India and Bangladesh. At the age of seventy, he started to doodle with erasures in his manuscripts that gradually evolved into paintings. In the last fifteen years of his life he produced more than a thousand paintings that are startling in their bold experimentation. His brilliance did not stop at the literary, the musical, or even the artistic; he was also a participant and leader in the social and political affairs of the world. In 1905, when the British divided Bengal into East and West Bengal, Rabindranath was at the helm of a protest movement called Swadeshi. He retired from active participation in politics when the movement turned violent. Building on this experience, he later wrote the novel *Home and the World* (adapted for the screen by Satyajit Ray) where, through the character of Nikhil, Rabindranath elaborated a social philosophy that Martha Nussbaum has recently called cosmopolitanism.[2] Never hesitant to act on his beliefs, Rabindranath renounced his knighthood in 1919 as a protest against the

Massacre of Amritsar perpetrated by the British. Perhaps the greatest achievement of Rabindranath as a man of action was the establishment of Visva-Bharati University in rural Bengal. In this institution, with its motto "the world in one nest," Rabindranath sought to build an educational program founded on the principle of international cultural exchange. He was perhaps the first educational thinker in the modern world who put into practice the notion that a complete education must be open to the diverse cultural heritages of the world. Figures such as Indira Gandhi (former prime minister of India), Satyajit Ray (world-renowned filmmaker), and Amartya Sen (Nobel Prize–winning philosopher-economist), among others, are products of Rabindranath's educational institution and philosophy.

III

While preparing to visit England in 1912, Rabindranath fell ill and had to cancel the trip. Convalescing in rural Bengal, he took to translating into English some of the religious poetry that he had recently published in Bengal. Eventually, he made the trip to England later in the same year and presented some of the English versions in a reading that was attended by a group of eminent cultural figures of London, including William Butler Yeats. A limited edition of these translations, *Gitanjali,* was published in London the same year with an introduction by Yeats. While Rabindranath in 1912 was already the leading literary figure in the Bengali language, he was almost unknown in the West. In 1913, only a year later, he was awarded the Nobel Prize in literature and became a world figure virtually overnight.

The world fame of Rabindranath in the post–Nobel Prize period of his life rested in part on translations made into many of the languages of the world. After *Gitanjali,* upon the insistence of his English publisher, Macmillan, Rabindranath himself produced several volumes of translations of his works. Most of the translations into other languages, both in Europe and Asia, were made from these English versions. In both these regions, Rabindranath remains to this day an important literary presence. The 1999 *Time* magazine poll of the twenty most influential Asians of the twentieth century includes Rabindranath as the only literary representative.[3] The influence of his works continues to proliferate in some parts of the world because great writers translated him: Juan Ramón Jiménez, Anna Akhmatova, André Gide, among others. They produced compelling presentations of Rabindranath's work (in Spanish, Russian, and French, respectively), even though these versions were made from the English editions, which did not sustain the power of Rabindranath's original Bengali. In the Anglophone world, however, there are no equivalent examples of powerful translations of Rabindranath's work for much of the twentieth century. Fortunately, more recently, a new generation of translators have taken up the challenge of re-presenting Rabindranath to the English-speaking world. In the 1980s and 1990s, William Radice, Ketaki Kushari Dyson, Krishna Dutta, and Andrew Robinson have contributed to the renewal of interest in Rabindranath by publishing some exciting volumes of translations made from the original Bengali. We hope that this selection from the final poems adds to the growing enthusiasm for Rabindranath's work among English speakers.

Indian writers who write in English are now celebrated. And rightly so: they are indeed fine writers. It is a mistake, however, to think that the handful of novels produced by this group exhaust the modern Indian literary tradition. The great literary traditions in the languages of India must be included in any understanding of modern Indian literature. In this respect, the achievements of Rabindranath Tagore are pivotal. Apart from his profound impact on the development of Bengali literature, his writings deeply influenced the modern literary traditions in the other languages of India as well. Rabindranath is indispensable to the reader interested in Indian literature.

We speakers of the Bengali language are always conscious of Rabindranath's legacy; for us the language as we know it is inconceivable without his writings. The Bengali believe that in Rabindranath's writings, especially in his poems and songs, every nuance of the human condition is recorded. In the Anglophone world, however, Rabindranath was stereotyped as a mystical poet, partly because the first wave of translations following the Nobel Prize concentrated only on his deeply theistic poems. Any one selection cannot do justice to the immense variety of poetry that Rabindranath wrote throughout his life. This collection brings together a selection from the very last phase of Rabindranath's poetry. Many more volumes of translations are needed to begin to mirror in English the range of his poetic achievements.

IV

The consciousness of death, which forms the horizon of the poems in this volume, was sadly all too present in the poet's life. In a series of tragedies, he lost his three children and wife. As the youngest of fourteen siblings, he bore the loss of most of his brothers and sisters. These harrowing experiences of recurring grief found expression in the poetry and song of the Tagorean oeuvre; in his work, the immense healing power of resignation is the one source of deep and lasting consolation. The poetry of *Gitanjali,* which captured the imagination of the West, evokes some of these grief-stricken moments, which none of us are spared. A letter received by Rabindranath in 1920 movingly relates the heart-wrenching pain of loss and attests to just how powerfully Rabindranath speaks to the experience of grief:

Dear Sir Rabindranath:
I have been trying to find courage to write to you ever since I heard that you were in London—but the desire to tell you something is finding its way into this letter today. The letter may never reach you, for I do not know how to address it, tho' I feel sure your name upon the envelope will be sufficient. It is nearly two years ago, that my dear eldest son went out to the War for the last time and the day he said Goodbye to me—we were looking together across the sun-glorified sea—looking towards France with breaking hearts—when he, my poet son, said these wonderful words of yours—beginning at 'When I go from hence, let this be my parting word'—and when his pocket book came back to me—I found these words

written in his dear writing—with your name beneath.
Would I be asking too much of you, to tell me what book
I should find the whole poem in?[4]

The letter was signed by Susan Owen, the mother of the British "war poet" Wilfred Owen.

The consoling power of Rabindranath's writings on death led Janusz Korczak, the legendary Polish educational thinker and activist, to produce Rabindranath's play *The Post Office* with the children of his orphanage in the Warsaw Ghetto. Two months later, Korczak and the children were taken away and gassed in Treblinka. When asked why he chose to stage *The Post Office,* Korczak reportedly responded by saying "because eventually one had to learn to accept serenely the angel of death."[5]

In his final poems, written after a major illness and with death beckoning, Rabindranath gives us in words the movement of his thoughts as *he* approaches death. There is no raging against the dying of the light, only an unadorned honesty intermittently lit by luminous memories.

V

This translation of a selection from Rabindranath's last four collections—*Sickbed, Recovery, On My Birthday,* and *Last Poems*—is motivated in part by a desire to understand the dramatic philosophical and poetic shift evident in these poems. They are, in fact, unlike anything Rabindranath had written before. Classical Indian thought—the intellectual tradition that Rabindranath was intimately acquainted with—can shed light on how these final poems represent a new horizon in his poetry.

It is well known that Rabindranath inherited from his father an abiding love for the Upanishads, one of the formative texts of the Hindu religion. In classical Indian thought, the Upanishadic doctrines were interpreted in differing ways by the three schools of Vedānta, an orthodox system of Hindu philosophy: Advaita (nondualism) of the philosopher Sankara, Visistadvaita (qualified nondualism) of Ramanuja, and Dvaita (dualism) of Madhva. For Sankara, *Brahman* (the highest reality of the Upanishads) transcends all possible conceptual-linguistic qualifications; as a consequence, *Brahman* cannot be revealed through language. In contrast, for Ramanuja, the world as experienced through our senses is a quality of *Brahman,* just as, say, colors are qualities of objects; and for Madhva *Brahman* is the god of monotheism. Ramanuja and Madhva, then, as opposed to Sankara, put forth versions of theism that admit the possibility of linguistic access into Being. (I am using the word *theism* to describe the view that encompasses the belief in the existence of either one or multiple personal deities.) Theism does not limit the possibilities of religious interpretations of reality; Buddhism, for instance, does not include the belief in a personal god. Similarly, Sankara, the philosopher of the Advaita school of Vedānta, rejects the view that ultimate reality is a personal deity, though for reasons different from those given by Buddhism. Rabindranath's own *Gītānjali, Gītāli,* and *Naibedya* (three collections of poetry), however, contained remarkable examples of devotional lyrics dedicated to a personal deity. The English-language edition of *Gītānjali,* which led to his being awarded the Nobel Prize, contained the poet's own translations of some of these *bhakti,* or devotional lyrics.

Rabindranath's conception of *jībandebatā* (life-god), following the theistic interpretation of the Upanishads, holds that the nature of Being can be disclosed through language. He identifies *jībandebatā* as the Poet and, therefore, language and poetry as the medium of ontological disclosure:

> To this Poet, who fashions my life out of all my good and bad, strong and weak points, I have given the name of *jīban-debatā* in my poetry. I do not just think that he forms all the separate fragments of my being into a unity, so as to bring it into consonance with the universe; I also believe he has brought me to this present life from some previous existence, via a strange stage of forgetfulness; and that a strong memory (derived from his power) of my flowing journey through the universe continues to remain subtly within me. That is why I feel so ancient a harmony with the trees and animals and birds of this world; that is why I do not find the vastness and mystery of the world either alien or terrifying.[6]

This anti-Advaitic position is further articulated in the Hibbert Lectures, which Rabindranath delivered at Oxford:

> According to some interpretations of the Vedanta doctrine Brahman is the absolute Truth, the impersonal It, in which there can be no distinction of this or that, the good and the evil, the beautiful and its opposite, having no other quality except its ineffable blissfulness. . . . But as our religion can only have its significance in the phenomenal world comprehended by our human self, this

absolute conception of Brahman is outside the subject of my discussion. . . . [W]hatever name may have been given to the divine Reality it has found its highest place in the history of our religion owing to its human character. . . .[7]

Jībandebatā brings about a synthesis between humanism and religious consciousness. This theme found philosophical resonance when, in a 1930 conversation with Albert Einstein on the nature of reality, Rabindranath remarked:

[T]here is the reality of the paper infinitely different from the reality of literature. For the kind of mind possessed by the moth which eats the paper, literature is absolutely non-existent, yet for Man's mind literature has a greater value of truth than the paper itself. In a similar manner, if there be some truth which has no sensuous or rational relation to the human mind it will ever remain as nothing so long as we remain human beings.[8]

In other words, Rabindranath is making the compelling claim that meaning is dependent upon the subject, while not denying that there is a world out there, independent of the subject. Such a claim strongly implies that language can illuminate the structure of Being. In the context of the present discussion, then, Rabindranath's literary odyssey can be understood as being underpinned by this essentially *theistic* gesture, with one major exception: the notion of *jībandebatā* cannot be used to interpret the poetry he wrote during the last year of his life.

These final poems, fraught with uncertainty, recognize instead that language, in the final analysis, cannot disclose Being. Within the context of classical Indian thought, such a recognition is essentially an Advaitic event. Of all the philosophical commentators of the Upanishads, Sankara most forcefully argued that language cannot pry open the hermetic structure of Being. The other great thinker from the Indian tradition who held a similar view regarding the relationship between language and Being was the great Buddhist thinker Nagarjuna, who, with the aid of a brilliant deconstructionist dialectic, affirmed that any and all judgments concerning the nature of Being are inherently unstable. These final poems shift dramatically away from implications of *jībandebatā* and *bhakti*-driven theism and align themselves with the Advaitic position that valorizes the note of Silence.

The first intimation of this profound philosophical change in Rabindranath's thinking can be traced to *On My Birthday* 20; here, he creates a remarkable image of language in the process of losing its power of signification and sharply criticizes the view that language can uncover the nature of Being:

> Today I imagine the words of countless
> Languages to be suddenly fetterless—
> After long incarceration
> In the fortress of grammar, suddenly up in rebellion.
> Maddened by the stamp-stamping
> Of unmitigated regimented drilling.
> They have jumped the constraints of sentence
> To seek free expression in a world rid of intelligence,
> Snapping the chains of sense in sarcasm
> And ridicule of literary decorum.
>
> . . . .

> the free-roving mind fashions
> Artistic creations
> Of a kind that do not conform to an orderly
> Universe—whose threads are tenuous, loose, arbitrary,
> Like a dozen puppies brawling,
> Scrambling at each other's necks to no purpose or meaning[9]

In another poem, *Recovery* 25, words invade the very process of writing; concealing rather than disclosing, they fail to reveal meaning:

> In vast consciousness,
> unuttered word clusters
> hurtle mute, through cycles of time
> like interstellar nebulae.
> Suddenly they break
> through my borders,
> freeze into forms,
> orbit the path of my writing.[10]

Rabindranath's final poems are replete with images of *bhāshāhīnatā*—the state of "languagelessness," of Silence. These poems enter a region of absolute and incorruptible honesty where, to (mis)use a phrase from Jean-François Lyotard, there is no attempt at presenting the unpresentable. The very unpresentability of Being, echoing the Rig Vedic Hymn to Creation, where the mystery of creation transcends the limits of words, becomes the stuff of poetry:

> The first day's sun
> questioned
> the new appearance of being—

Who are you?
There was no answer.

Years went by.
Day's last sun
asked the last question from the shores of the west
in the soundless evening—
Who are you?
There was no answer.[11]

The theism implied by the notion of *jībandebatā,* which was the poet's voice of disclosure, is completely left behind in these words. Here, the ultimate concealment of Being from the gaze of language is celebrated.

William Radice, commenting on *On My Birthday* 20 in his translation of a selection of Rabindranath's poetry, suggests that this poem "comes perilously *close* to acceptance of a complete lack of meaning or purpose in the universe: to a suspicion that, though there may be laws or rules governing Nature or the mind of man, their status may be frivolous and arbitrary as the rules of a game."[12] I would say, rather, that in his later poetry Rabindranath no longer has confidence in the power of language to reveal the nature of meaning. The recognition that Being escapes the limning power of language does not logically imply metaphysical nihilism.

The poetry of Silence practices the art of dying, which Plato acknowledged as the highest craft, an event viewed as a singular act of disclosing reality. Moreover, the poetry of Silence conveys a deep implication for the evolution of Rabindranth's religious consciousness. The absolute Silence invoked by the sun (*rabi,* the first part of the compound noun *rabindra,* means "sun") cannot be understood in theistic terms. These unadorned words gather their poetic power in their attempt to penetrate a deeper, transtheistic articulation of Being, *only to recognize that such a revelation is not possible.* This recognition at times inspires terror, as in *Last Poems* 4, which is dedicated to the empty chair from Argentina (a gift from Victoria Ocampo):

> As a lost dog looks up with sad eyes,
> the numb mind's pain questions,
> What has happened? Why it happened is unknown.
> Day and night, useless eyes search everywhere
> The words of the chair more fragile, mournful.
> Silent pain of emptiness fill this loveless room.[13]

More often the realization that revelation of Being through poetry is impossible calls forth a moving humanity as in *Last Poems* 10, where death and the state of languagelessness become intertwined:

> Today my sack is empty.
> I have given completely
> whatever I had to give.
> In return if I receive anything—
> some love, some forgiveness—
> then I will take it with me
> when I step on the boat that crosses
> to the festival of the wordless end.[14]

A profound silence—an utter sense of stillness—radiates from these images.

The sentiments of the condolence letter quoted at the beginning of this introduction, tender and simple, spring from an understanding of both finitude and transcendence, from the experience of a poet approaching his death. These final poems, Rabindranath's letters to himself, transform his experience into words—words that approach the absolute terrain of wordlessness.

—SARANINDRANATH TAGORE

Notes

1. *Selected Letters of Rabindranath Tagore,* ed. Krishna Dutta and Andrew Robinson (Cambridge: Cambridge University Press, 1997), p. 526.

2. Martha Nussbaum discusses the novel in "Patriotism and Cosmopolitanism" in *For Love of Country,* ed. Joshua Cohen (Boston: Beacon Press, 1996).

3. *Time* (Asian edition), August 1999.

4. Krishna Dutta and Andrew Robinson, *Rabindranath Tagore: The Myriad-Minded Man* (London: Bloomsbury, 1995), p. 2.

5. Ibid., p. 3.

6. As cited in William Radice's introduction to *Rabindranath Tagore, Selected Short Stories,* trans. William Radice (Harmondsworth: Penguin Books, 1991), p. 17.

7. Rabindranath Tagore, *The Religion of Man* (London: Unwin, 1958), pp. 127–28.

8. *A Tagore Reader,* ed. Amiya Chakravarty (Boston: Beacon Press, 1961), p. 112.

9. *Rabindranath Tagore, Selected Poems,* trans. William Radice (Harmondsworth: Penguin Books, 1985), p. 124.

10. From *Recovery* 25, translation by Wendy Barker and Saranindranath Tagore.

11. From *Last Poems* 13, translation by Wendy Barker and Saranindranath Tagore.

12. From William Radice's introduction in *Rabindranath Tagore, Selected Poems,* p. 39.

13. From *Last Poems* 4, translation by Wendy Barker and Saranindranath Tagore.

14. From *Last Poems* 10, translation by Wendy Barker and Saranindranath Tagore.

RABINDRANATH TAGORE

Final Poems

FROM

Sickbed

Sickbed 5

Under this vast universe
pain's mill-wheel rotates,
grinds planets and stars to powder.
Sparks flash, scatter
suffering on every side,
ash-webs from annihilated worlds
permeating in an instant.
In the mills of oppression,
in cells of luminous consciousness,
pikes and knives clank,
wound-blood spurts.
The tiny human body—
infinite, its power to face pain.
In the assembly of creation and annihilation,
this small vessel of blood
offered to the Tantric circle
reels, drunken, rapturous.
The clay cup of the body fills
with incoherent blood, floods with tears.
Every moment unfolds unending
worth to consciousness, invincible.
The body's pain-hallowed fire,
the offering sacrificed
to ascetic acts of stars,

is incomparable.
Such enduring vigor,
compassion without fear,
indifference to death,
such triumphant processions:
assemblies trampling beds of flame
to find pain's limits—
on a fevered, unnamed pilgrimage,
together, from path to path,
penetrating caves of fire, to find care's origins,
provisions of unending love.

4 November 1940

Sickbed 7

Deep night-interior,
beneath the patient's clouded sight,
when I see
your wakened presence,
the sky's uncounted planet-suns
in limitless time
greet my mortality.
After, when I know
you will go,
terror swells
from the apathy of the world's vast silence.

12 November 1940 (2:00 a.m.)

Sickbed 9

Ancient dark-swept night:
in this illness-soaked shadow,
in my mind
you sit contemplating creation
in time's first eon, in dense blackness,
utterly alone,
mute, blind.
I see
my own painful attempts to create
in that beginningless sky.
A maimed cry wells from a bottomless sleep—
the urge to express the self
seeps from wombs of steel,
secretly leaps into flame.
Unintending, your finger
weaves the veiling art of maya.
Suddenly, from the vast old ocean-womb,
rise great heaps of dreams,
incomplete, indistinct,
waiting in darkness
to receive their bodies from time's right hand.
Under a new sun

the deformed will assume harmonious shapes.
The creator of forms will come to chant mantras—
slowly, the strands of the Sacred's hidden plan will stream,
    will be revealed.

13 November 1940 (morning)

Sickbed 13

If the long painful night
ends its ferrying
on the farthest shore of the past,
then in the center of a new wonder,
in a child's playground of worlds,
in that dawn, wakes
life's new question.
With no answers to old questions,
people jeer
at stumped minds,
the way children do, thoughtlessly playing games.
The answer I receive
I accept in simple faith,
faith that stays satisfied,
uncontending,
bringing truth—a trust, a joy.

15 November 1940

Sickbed 17

I dozed off,
woke, and saw
by my feet
a basket of oranges
someone had brought.
The mind sends
guesses that return
one by one, gentle names.
I know—or maybe I don't—
that with the one unknown,
many names meet
from many directions.
In one name all become true—
giving brings
utter content.

21 November 1940

Sickbed 21

Waking in the morning,
I saw a rose in my vase,
and wondered—
in the cycle of ages,
what force brought it to this peak of beauty,
side-stepping pits of imperfection?
Was it blind, forgetful, like the ones who renounce the world,
not distinguishing beauty from ugliness?
Was it strictly logical? Material?
Nothing of the spirit?
Some argue that in the congress of creation
beauty and ugliness sit equally.
Neither is kept out.
I am a poet—I won't take sides.
I see the world whole,
the billions of planets and stars in the sky
balancing vast beauty.
Their rhythms are not tripped, their songs are not choked.
Distortions cause no lapses.
In the sky I see layer upon layer, petals spreading
a luminous, vast rose.

24 November 1940 (morning)

Sickbed 23

Recovering, welcomed
again by life's calm
that offers me
cleansed eyes to see the world.
Blue sky diffused with light, morning—
ancient yogi's
clearing of mind—
I open
to the unending moment
of Brahma's awakening.
I know my own birth
is woven with new ones.
As with a constellation's light of suns
this vision carries
unseen, untold streams—all creation.

25 November 1940 (morning)

Sickbed 26

I have no faith in my works.
I know time's ocean,
its lashings of waves, day by day
will erase them.
My faith is in my self.
The whole day I fill my cup and drink
the perpetual nectar of this world.
Every moment's love
has been saved in it.
The weight of pain has not torn
and dust has not blackened
its art.
I know,
when I go from
the play of this life,
the forests of flower, every season, will witness
I have loved the world.
Only this love is real, gift of my birth.
When I say farewell
this undecaying truth will cancel death.

28 November 1940 (morning)

Sickbed 27

Open the door,
let the blue sky span wide,
let inquisitive scents of petals enter my room,
let the first sunlight
seep through the veins of my body.
In the rustling of leaves let me hear
words that greet my being alive.
Let this morning
cover my mind with its shawl
as it shelters the new grass of the dark field.
All the love I have received—
its wordlessness
I hear in the sky, in the wind.
Today I bathe in its ceremony, its sacred waters.
The truth of a whole life as a gemmed garland
I see on the breast of that blue.

28 November 1940 (morning)

Sickbed 35

As after a wind storm
the breast of the sky opens
a path of luminous dawn
deep, silent, blue—
may my life be free
of the past with its net of fog.
May a wakening conch sound
at the door of this birth.
I am waiting.
May smudges be erased from the light,
may the futile race end, turning me into play.
May a love unclinging
receive its final value from its own giving self.
In this aging current, when I float in the dark and light
from bank to bank, may I not glance back
to my past acts again and again.
Let me place the layer upon layer
of suffering and unending joy
on a level plane with other floating events, tens of millions,
let me look at them wantless, terrorless
in exile without relations.
This is my last word:
let endless whiteness complete my presence.

3 December 1940 (morning)

Sickbed 37

One day, I saw, in an ashen moment of dusk,
death's right hand entangling life's throat
tied with offered threads of blood;
I recognized you both.
I saw the wedding gift:
the groom's final offering to the bride,
streaming from the right hand to the end of age.

4 December 1940 (morning)

Sickbed 39

When I don't see you, pain weaves
a world under me that whispers
your leaving.
Panicked, I try to seize an emptying sky
with stretched hands.
The dream breaks.
And there you are, knitting,
beside me—
bending to the calm of creation.

5 December 1940 (morning)

FROM

Recovery

Recovery 3

Empty patient's room.
Through the open door
shadow has fallen slant on the bed.
Afternoon winter warmth, sleepy day,
sluggish, a mossy river.
Moment by moment the past rises, breathes
in these barren fields.

I remember those days:
under crumbling banks the River Padma
in shadow, light,
floats wandering thoughts
foam to foam
into this old morning.
At the edge of emptiness,
a boat sail spreading,
clouds straggling in a corner of sky.
Sun-dazzled urns balanced on their waists, village girls'
whispers under saris pulled over their heads
echo the path, winding. In the shadows of mango groves,
cuckoo songs, somewhere from the branches.
Shadowed rhythm of village-life—
its fabric of mystery—I tremble.

The yellow-gold mustard fields by the ponds:
earth's gifts to the flow of light.
At the feet of the sun's temple, offerings of blossom.

This quiet time of day
my stilled vision sends soundless chants
to the Sacred, in whose luminousness the original one
saw the form of the gods.
If the sounds of the oldest mantras were in my voice,
my hymns would vanish in this translucent light, light.
No words. No words.
I see into the distance where edges dissolve
my silence as a canopy in the white blueness of noon sky.

1 February 1941 (afternoon)

Recovery 4

A bell rings in the distance
and the city's cloud-scraping self-announcing
chatter vanishes from the mind.
In sun-warmed winter light, for no reason, images emerge
neglected at the edges of life's travels.

A field-path threading villages wanders far off
by the riverbanks.
Under an ancient fig tree
people are waiting for the ferry
beside their market wares.
In a tin-roofed village hut—
jaggery jars lined in rows,
neighborhood dogs' greedy tongues,
flies crowding.
A cart on the road
heavy-loaded with jute.
Sacks dragged, one by one, weighed, voices shrill
behind the warehouse.
Untied oxen
return from munching grass by the path,
tail-whips lashing their backs.
Piles of mustard

wait for the storehouse.
A fishing boat docks,
fisherwomen gather, baskets in the crooks of their arms—
a hawk flies overhead.
Side by side, merchant boats tied on the steep bank.
In the sun, on rooftops, oarsmen mend nets.
Hugging the necks of their buffalo, farmers float across
to the rice fields on the other side.
In the distance, above the forest-line, a temple crest
shimmers in the morning sun.
At invisible edges of fields—a train
stretches dim, dimmer
sound-lines across the breast of the wind,
smoke trailing
a long flag vanquishing distance.

I remember—nothing much—long ago
in deepest night,
a boat tied to the banks of the Ganges.
Polished water at dusk,
shadow-shapes thickening hushed forest edges,
lamp flames through cracks in the woods.
Suddenly I wake.
In the wordless night sky
a song lifts from a young voice.
A slim boat rushes on the ebbing current,
disappears.
On both banks by the forest, a shiver keeps vigil—
sculpted stillness of a moon-crowned night,
silence on my mat of broken sleep.

The west bank of the Ganges—a house at the edge of town.
The shallows stretch into distance,
emptiness under a blank sky.
A few cows graze in a harvested millet field.
Farmer boys, with their sticks, fend goats
from melon tendrils.
Somewhere, from a village, a woman by herself,
a basket in her arm, walks off to find spinach.
And always, down by the line of the river
in a row, bent-backed, slow-pulling oarsmen.
In the water, on land, all day, no other signs of life.
Nearby in the garden, neglected, a flowering tree
beside a grand old neem tree, a bench embedded in its trunk,
its dense aristocratic shadow
at night a shelter for egrets.
Well water
gurgles all day through the canal
to feed the corn crop.
Someone is singing, grinding wheat,
jingling bracelets of brass.
The noon is enfolded by one melody repeating.

These path-meetings while walking,
little moments, wake
at the edges of consciousness.
All these neglected images,
life's last dividing pains,
arrive with the far tolling of the bell.

31 January 1941 (evening)

Recovery 6

Distant, fragile, pale blue of sky
above the forest trees lifting
their arms, a silent offering of green.
Winter's tender sun on earth
spreads a shawl of clear light.
I am writing this down before
the painter, indifferent, wipes clean the canvas.

24 January 1941 (morning)

Recovery 7

Cruel night sneaks in, breaks
the locks of my weakened body,
penetrates, and takes my pride.
The mind falls to attacks of black.
But as the insult of defeat and shame
of such weariness well up, suddenly
where distant edges meet, day's flag
shimmers gold threading
from a distant point of sky,
sounding "a lie, a lie."
In the serene morning light I see myself
as one who has conquered suffering
at the peak of this old body's citadel.

27 January 1941 (morning)

Recovery 8

Alone by sorrow's last window.
The far blue edges——a language of endlessness.
Shadow-threaded, light
streams from the rain trees, a green friend.
Not far, not very far——rings in the mind.
The path melts behind the mound of the setting sun.
I am silent by the inn's door of dusk
that lights from time to time
the temple crest of the last pilgrimage.
There by the gate swells the *rāginī* of twilight,
spiraling all that is beautiful of this birth,
all that has touched my being, my travels,
this hint of fullness.
Not far, not very far, rings in the mind.

3 February 1941 (evening)

Recovery 9

In the space of vast creation:
play of fireworks sky across sky,
with suns and stars
from age to the end of age.
I too have come from the beginningless invisible
with a tiny dot at the end of the spark
to this corner, this little place, this bit of time.
As I have arrived at this act of departure
the flame of the lamp fades.
In the shadow, the maya-form of this play,
happiness, sadness, these theatrical clothes
fall slowly away.
I see ages through ages, the hundreds upon hundreds of players
discarding their colored garments
outside the doors of the playhouse.
I see
beyond the hundreds upon hundreds of extinguished stars
the Dancing Lord, alone, silent.

3 February 1941 (evening)

Recovery 14

Daily, in the morning, this faithful dog,
silent, sits near me,
till I recognize him
with a touch.
At my little notice
his body erupts in waves, streams of joy.
In the wordless world of life
this single creature,
beyond good or evil,
sees the complete human being—
who springs to life in delight,
into whom can be poured limitless, reasonless love,
whose consciousness shows the path
in unending worlds of sentience.
When I see this mute creature's
utter surrender,
revealing all his limitations,
I cannot quite understand what value he has found,
through his simple awareness, in the human form;
his wordless sight, sad, perplexed
cannot tell what it understands—
yet lets me know what it means to be human in the swirl
     of the universe.

22 December 1940 (morning)

Recovery 22

Distant Himalayas' orange groves'
vessels of juice
bring to my bedside
a secluded morning's closeness of sun;
unknown waterfalls'
diffused light-lines'
letters of gold;
and thick forest-edges'
soundless murmur-wrapped
calming signature.
In private language, illness maimed,
the poet signs his blessing.

25 November 1940

Recovery 24

This lazy bed, languorous life
makes art of tangles of moss—
fameless, limitless—it speaks
the names of life's little worth.

23 January 1941 (morning)

Recovery 25

In vast consciousness,
unuttered word clusters
hurtle mute, through cycles of time
like interstellar nebulae.
Suddenly they break
through my borders,
freeze into forms,
orbit the path of my writing.

5 December 1940 (morning)

Recovery 30

Dusk drops down slowly—bindings loosed one by one
from the work-nets of hours. Day casts
the west's opening portal
into gold-luminous darkness, meeting space of seas.
Silent, obeisant, head bent to the far dawn,
eyelids lower—the time has come
to lose one's name
beneath the floor of consciousness.
In those endless skies where star-etched fields of peace
stretch across unformed seeds of day—
there to receive one's own worth,
asail in the night's ocean.

16 February 1941 (afternoon)

Recovery 3 I

From time to time I feel the moment for travel has come.
On the day of leaving, cast a veil
of humble sunset-glaze.
Let the time to leave
be quiet, still. Let no pompous memorials
build the hypnosis of grieving.
Let the lines of trees by the departure door
bestow the tranquil chanting of earth
on quiet heaps of leaves.
Let night's soundless blessing slowly descend,
iridescent offerings of the seven stars.

Written sometime between 22 December 1940 and 2 January 1941

FROM

On My Birthday

On My Birthday 5

As I enter my eightieth year,
wonder rises
at the hundreds of millions of stars'
fire-fall of silent floods
streaming at ineffable speeds through unknown emptiness
in all directions.
In that darkness-packed, limitless breast of sky
suddenly I burst
like a momentary spark from the fires of the endless universe
into the histories of centuries' successions.
I have entered that world where eons upon eons
rise from wombs of life-silted seas
under vast inertness beneath,
disclosing my hidden, astonishing presence
branching into forms, transfigured forms.
Incomplete being's illusion-entwined shadow
that has blanketed for ages the animal world—
for whom does it wait so attentively?
After uncountable days and nights,
human beings slowly
enter the stage of life.
One by one, new lights gleam,
new meanings gather words.

In this strange light
humans see their exquisite future form,
in the world's theater,
slowly, act by act, signs of consciousness.
Along with rest of the cast,
I have worn my costume.
I too was called to help raise the curtain.
Astonishing!
How fertile, our earth, mortal place for souls.
Around me, in the sky, in light, in the wind,
under earth, oceans, the mountains—
what deep design is carried, orbiting the sun?
Stitched with this thread of mystery I arrived eighty years ago.
A little later, I will leave.

5 May 1940

On My Birthday 7

In the afternoon, invited to the birthday,
the mountain dwellers arrived.
Bowing, palms pressed, one by one
they presented me with flowers.
To receive the earth in a moment,
resting on a stone bench——
blessings after years of burning austerity,
these gifts of blossoms——
hope of consecrating every human birth.
That boon, benediction for the human condition
came to my hands today
on my birthday——a resonant memory.
In star-etched space,
somewhere in the midst of a bank of light,
sometimes, such rare, astonishing homage.

6 May 1940

On My Birthday 8

Ripping the breast off my birthday
today, news of the death, leave-taking of a friend, has arrived.
My own fire-grief burns—
enkindles.
On evening's forehead, the sun places
a blood-gleaming sign,
changes the coming night's face to gold
just as death dresses me with a burning flame
at the western edge of life.

In this light can be seen
seamless life where birth, death are one.
Such splendor illuminates a deathlessness
hidden in the everyday by our senses' limits.

6 May 1940

On My Birthday 11

Like clusters of foam
whipped by time's vortex—
this maya, shaded in light, in darkness—
the bodiless becomes material.
My being—from where I don't know—
rises, a swift-running current.
Suddenly, inconceivably,
from an unseen origin, the center forms itself.
The world's soul peeks through:
behind this jest, an unknown jokester.
The infinite's play with a freckle of time
knits openings to closings,
luminous rhythms.
A speck of time appears, hidden as a veiled bride,
dressed in garlands
of effervescent gems.
She takes her place at the center of creation.
Within cells of the self, the infinite tells of its presence.

2 May 1940

On My Birthday 14

In the mountain's blue and the horizon's blue—
mantras, rhythms of air and earth.
Forests are washed in fall's gold-shadowed sun.
Butterflies—purple as eggplants—look for honey in the
    yellow flowers.
In the midst of all this, I am.
That is why from every side, in silence, the hand-clapping
    of skies.
My joy is jumbled with these colors, these songs—
is this known in Kalimpong?

In their treasure chests the mountain peaks store
the endless ages.
This day-garland of joy is placed
to spread the celebration
in unplayed tunes
farther and farther,
across the spaces between stars.
This morning the gold bell rings—dong, dong, dong.
Is it heard in Kalimpong?

25 September 1940

On My Birthday 21

Brutal war's blood-stained teeth
rip the intestines
from hundreds of villages and cities.
Reasonless menace spreads in every direction.
A flood descends from the House of Death,
apocalyptic tides erode the shores of nations and empires.
The passions of greed—
teams of trained hunters, domesticated carnivores,
over ages and distances—
wound the flesh of country after country.
Those blinded gluttonous dogs tear at their chains,
forgetting even their own kind.
Primal cruelty unwraps its claws,
rips the pages of ancient traditions,
drops on every letter
the mud-covered traces of rot.
Messengers of discontented gods,
centuries of hoarded evil,
scatter across boundaries,
break the vats of those blind drunk on nationhood
out by the garbage dumps.
Crowds null their members' existences,
have sabotaged the sacred design
throughout history.

With that sin, curse of suicide, they are practicising cataclysm.
This merciless raging enemy
pulverizes even
its own gluttonous hedonists'
storeroom walls.

Wandering through the pyres of death,
Chinnamasta, severed head in her hand,
shatters human dreams in an instant,
swallows her own blood in a hundred streams.
When this hideous cosmic play concludes
in a horror-filled frenzied dance,
this evil age will end.
Simply clothed, human beings
will approach the ash-beds of cremation pyres.
They will sit on the seat of a new creation
with minds unmoved, unattached,
welcoming the new cannon booms.

22 May 1940

On My Birthday 24

Run-down house, deserted courtyard—
mute memory's silent cry whispers,
foundation's darkness, coffins of dead days,
well up in the voices of ghosts all afternoon.
Dry leaves whirlpool across fields,
the winds wheezing.
A sudden rainstorm hurls
savagery on the paths of departing March days.

Pangs of creation collide
behind the brush of the painter.
The pain of form
blooms into line after line
with the flaming red of a fragmented mind.
Sometimes a wayward stone jars the sweep of the brush.
Under the sheen of a hazy sky, in the neighboring lane,
cascading jangles of alarm
may suddenly sound
as the fingertips begin their intoxicated dance.
In vermilion shades of evening—
fireworks' explosions of madness.
The painter's brush is blocked, unblocked,
a paralysis at times caused by the cruel, the profane,
or simply by drunken incoherence.

In my mind the tides of turbid currents swell,
float away foaming irrelevence.
The maker of forms, in a form-heaped boat,
crosses the upstream night to suddenly looming banks.
Right and left, in-tune, out-of-tune, the splashing of oars
keeps beat to the painter's meditation, play of immersion.

25 February 1939

On My Birthday 26

From the vase one by one
life-seeped rose petals fall and fall.
In the world of blossoms
I do not see the crookedness of death.
The unbeautiful does not hurl mockeries at life.
The blossom does not profane with hate
its obligation to the soil;
in form, smell, a faded remainder is returned.
It holds the pained touch of farewell,
no rebuke.
When birthday, deathday are face-to-face
I see in that meeting
the hills of sunrise and sunset
trade glances with this parting day,
radiant dignity's obeisant, exquisite ending.

22 February 1941

On My Birthday 27

This world's vast nest,
night—its silent gestures
that steer the movements of the universe.
On all sides an ashened screen descends.
I tell myself, I will go home,
but where home is, I don't know.
Evening opens the door, alone,
to a poreless dark.
Hidden behind all light
the bearer of forgetfulness
takes away these costumes borrowed from earth,
makes perpetual
these tattered, aged, fading habits.
Immersion in the dark
cleanses new life's naked beginnings.
Here in the final regions of life,
on the last pathway of mystery
is freed a new mystery of creation.
I name a new birthday:
an awakening into light from night's mantras of the dark.

21 February 1941 (late evening)

On My Birthday 28

This river-tended life.
Many gifts from mountain peaks
move through its veins,
many strains of village soil layer its fields.
From many sides, life's fluid mystery
streams from grain to grain.
From east and west, many song-weavings
surround its awakening from dream.
The world's river-messenger
that brings the far near,
that brings to the door a welcome of the unknown,
has formed my birthday.
Carried by its current always
untethered, my moving nest
floats from bank to bank.
I am an outcast, a nomad.
Many grains of flowing hospitality
over and over, fill my birthday bowl.

23 February 1941 (afternoon)

FROM

Last Poems

Last Poems 2

Death-eclipse, that demon
lowering shadows
cannot devour life's sacred nectar
into the clutches of matter.
This I know for certain.
No thugs live in Earth's caves, tunnels,
who can defraud
love's ultimate worth.
This I know for certain.
The one I received as most true
disguised the most false.
This stain of being
won't be borne by the laws of the universe.
This I know for certain.
All things move through flux.
Such is the rule of time.
Death appears as fixed,
which is why in this world it is false.
This I know for certain.
He who knows the world as being
is me: I am
the witness of existence.
In the truth of the I lies the truth of being.
This I know for certain.

7 May 1940

55

Last Poems 4

Sun-heat drones
this afternoon alone.
A glance at the empty chair—
there is no comfort
in its breast full
of words of despair, weeping.
Words of emptiness rise, compassion-filled,
a meaning beyond understanding.
As a lost dog looks up with sad eyes,
the numb mind's pain questions,
What has happened? Why it happened is unknown.
Day and night, useless eyes search everywhere.
The words of the chair grow more fragile, mournful.
Silent pain of emptiness fills this loveless room.

26 March 1941 (evening)

Last Poems 10

I'm lost in the middle of my birthday.
I want my friends,
their touch,
with the earth's last love.
I will take life's final offering,
I will take the last human blessing.
Today my sack is empty.
I have given completely
whatever I had to give.
In return if I receive anything—
some love, some forgiveness—
then I will take it with me
when I step on the boat that crosses
to the festival of the wordless end.

6 May 1941 (morning)

Last Poems 13

The first day's sun
questioned
the new appearance of being—
Who are you?
There was no answer.

Years went by.
Day's last sun
asked the last question from the shores of the west
in the soundless evening—
Who are you?
There was no answer.

27 July 1941 (morning)

Last Poems 14

Sorrow's dark night over and over
has come to my door.
Its only visible weapons—
pain's deformed poses, fear's monstrous forms—
play out their deceptions in darkness.

When I have believed in the mask of fright,
I have faced empty defeat.
This game of win and lose—the sorcery of lies—
from childhood every step entangled in this dream of horror,
filled with sorrow's mockery.
Fear's strange and shifting cinema—
the skilled art of death dispersed through the dark.

29 July 1941 (evening)

NOTES ON THE POEMS

Rather than provide detailed explanations or interpretations, these notes are designed to convey a few points of clarification and context that will, we hope, enrich the reader's encounter with the poems. For those who wish to follow the chronology of the poems in relation to the day that Rabindranath passed on, please note that he died on 7 August 1941. Not all the poems appear chronologically, though all of them, except one, were written during the years of 1940 and 1941. Their order of appearance follows that of the original Bengali editions published by Visva-Bharati University Press. The date and time of composition of the poems, provided in the Bengali editions, are given at the end of each poem. The poems were written in either Shanti-niketan, where Rabindranath founded Visva-Bharati University, or in Jorasanko, the neighborhood in Calcutta where the ancestral mansion of the Tagores is situated. The only exceptions are *On My Birthday* 5, 7, 14, and 21, which were written in the eastern Himalayan regions.

FROM *Sickbed*
Sickbed 5

The images of cosmic violence in this poem stem from the poet's distress at the political situation of the world. A lifelong proponent of international cooperation, Rabindranath was shattered by the outbreak of World War II. His anguish over the war added to his physical pain throughout the last year and a half of his life. Rabindranath was deeply moved when told that on the night before the fall of Paris, a French radio station broadcast his play *The Post Office* in André Gide's translation. His final response to the brutality unleashed in Europe is famously recorded in the final address to his students in Shantiniketan. Since he was too weak to read it himself, "Sabhyatār Sankat" ("Crisis in Civilization") was read aloud in his presence. The final lines of the address affirm his faith in humanity, despite its capacity for brutality:

> And yet I shall not commit the grievous sin of losing faith in Man. I would rather look forward to the opening of a new chapter in his history after the cataclysm is over and the atmosphere is rendered clean with the spirit of service and sacrifice. Perhaps that dawn will come from this horizon, from the East where the sun rises. A day will come when unvanquished Man will retrace his path of conquest, despite all barriers, to win back his lost human heritage.

Line 16: "Tantric circle" (*bhairabī-chakra*). *Tantric* is the adjective form of *tantra,* the esoteric practice in Hinduism that *may* involve animal sacrifices and drinking of consecrated liquor. The ultimate goal of the practitioner of tantra is spiritual liberation. This term is untranslatable, but the hope is that it has some resonance in the English language owing to the sustained influence of Asian religions on Anglo-American culture. *Chakra* refers to a circular form, suggestive of the practice of sitting in a circle during rituals.

Sickbed 7

Line 11: "apathy" (*udasīn*). *Udasīn* also evokes the figure of a spiritual seeker who is indifferent toward the affairs of the world. In this sense, the last line becomes self-reflexive: the apathy of the world's silence enfolds the poet as well as the world.

Sickbed 9

Line 16: "maya." A Sanskrit word (the language in which classical Indian philosophy and poetry were written), *māyā* is part of the Bengali language along with many other Sanskrit words (Sanskrit and modern Northern Indian languages are, in fact, closely related). Like *kārmā,* it is a word familiar to English-language speakers. Leaving aside the philosophical significance of the term, *māyā* has come to mean "unreal" or "illusory" in English parlance. To say that the world is *māyā* would mean roughly that the world is unreal. In Indian philosophy, the notion of *māyā* is a philosophically charged concept, and it becomes deeply problematic to reduce it to unreality without some commentary. To take just one example: Sankara, the philosopher of the Advaita (nondual) Vedānta, considered the world of our everyday cognitions to be *māyā* but included that very world in the realm of Being. Thus *māyā* cannot mean absolute unreality. However, for Sankara, only *Brahman* (the deepest layer of reality as posited in the Upanishads) is absolutely real. Therefore, the world becomes unreal only from the perspective of a higher experience, the experience of *Brahman.* According to this view, the world is not unreal but rather as *māyā* it veils the absolute reality of *Brahman.*

Sickbed 13

Line 13: "simple faith" (*sahaj biśhās*). Faith here is not to be understood as religious faith but more as items of belief that a child assumes without questioning.

Line 7: "guesses" (*anumān*). The word can mean a guess implying uncertainty; but it can also mean a deduction implying certainty.

Sickbed 21

Line 10: "spirit" (*bodh*). *Bodh* is often translated as "intelligence," "understanding," or "sense." However, *bodh* is not ordinary intelligence or ordinary understanding; it implies a deep intuitive faculty that cannot be explained purely on naturalistic grounds. In other words, knowing through *bodh* is holistic (see line 15), qualitatively different from the analysis of argumentative rationality.

Sickbed 23

Line 10: "Brahma's awakening" (*kalpa-ārāmbha*). Radhakrishnan, the eminent philosopher, in *Indian Philosophy* (Dehli: Oxford University Press, 1996) writes, "the universe once created persists through an entire *kalpa,* or world period, after which it returns to the Supreme God, only to issue again from him" (p. 514). The notion of *kalpa* implies an oscillating universe, much like some versions of the Big Bang cosmology, in which the universe is created, destroyed, and re-created in endless cycles. The beginning of a *kalpa* marks the awakening of Brahma, the god of creation. *Ārāmbha,* the second part of this term, means "beginning."

FROM *Recovery*

Recovery 3

Line 9: "River Padma" (*padmā*). Rabindranath in his thirties worked as a manager of his family estates by the Padma. He lived and traveled in a houseboat, and it was during this time that he wrote some of his great short stories. Some of these stories appear in *Rabindranath Tagore, Selected Short Stories,* trans. William Radice (Harmondsworth: Penguin Books, 1991).

Line 30: "oldest mantras" (*Baidik mantra*). The obvious translation of this phrase would be "Vedic mantra" or "mantras." The Vedas are the oldest and most sacred texts of Hinduism. *Mantra* has become a part of English vocabulary; in English usage, however, the word has been thoroughly secularized, losing its sacred association, which is not the case in the Indic languages.

Recovery 8

Line 10: "*rāginī.*" Raga, melodic patterns that form the structure of improvisation in Indian classical music, is a word well known to the Anglophone reader. More technically, though, there are six ragas and thirty-six *rāginīs* in the original taxonomy. All the other patterns, numbering in the thousands, derive from the originals. *Rāginī* is the feminine form of *rāgā*.

Recovery 9

Line 18: "Dancing Lord" (*Natarāj*). *Natarāj* is one of the forms of Siva, the god of destruction in the Hindu trinity. In the form of *Natarāj,* a key element in Hindu iconography, Siva is portrayed dancing the dance of destruction (*tāndavnritya*).

Recovery 24

Line 3: "fameless, limitless" (*marjādā nāika*). This is a phrase full of semantic tension. *Marjādā* can mean both "prestige" or "honor," as well as "limit." *Nāika* brings in the negative form of the word. That which is prestigeless (fameless) can also be limitless.

Recovery 30

Line 7: "name" (*bājjha paricai*). Indian philosophical systems that derive from the Upanishads make a distinction between the phenomenal self that is part of the world and a transcendental self that grounds the self of empirical cognitions. The latter is *Atman,* the subject of much of Indian metaphysics. The name of an individual suggests the empirically driven self of psychology and does not describe the self at the deeper level. *Bājjha paricai* signifies the empirical self, which is why we use the word "name."

Line 8: "floor of consciousness" (*dhyān*). *Dhyān* is a form of deep meditation that allows the seeker in Hindu tradition to discover the structural depths of consciousness not available to everyday cognitions.

Recovery 31

Line 11: "seven stars" (*Saptarshi*). Literally, "seven saints" or the constellation Ursa Major.

FROM *On My Birthday*
On My Birthday 5

Rabindranath had a lifelong interest in the sciences and on more than one occasion had (recorded) philosophical exchanges with his friend Albert Einstein (see *A Tagore Reader,* ed. Amiya Chakravarty [Boston: Beacon Press, 1961] and "Portfolio: Einstein and Tagore," *The Kenyon Review* [vol. 23, no. 2, 2001]). Late in life, well into his seventies, Rabindranath wrote *Biswa Parichai,* translated as *Our Universe,* which was written to introduce young readers to the excitement of science in general and the wonders of the new physics in particular. Some of the images in this poem display Rabindranath's interest in evolutionary biology, as well as his legendary interest in the theater (see also *Recovery 9*). He not only wrote a few dozen plays, he acted in them as well in Calcutta productions. Some of them were staged in the Tagore mansion, with other members of the family in the cast. Rabindranath's plays continue to be a staple for the vibrant theater community of Calcutta.

On My Birthday 7

This poem (as well as *On My Birthday 5*, 8, and 11) was written in Mongpu, a hill station in the eastern Himalayas near Darjeeling. Rabindranath spent the days around his penultimate birthday as a guest of the family of Maitreyi Devi, whose father, the famous historian of Indian philosophy, Surendranath Dasgupta, was a friend of the Tagores'. Maitreyi Devi would later win fame with her novel (written as a response to Mircea Eliade's autobiography *Bengal Nights*), *Na Hanayate,* translated as *It Does Not Die* (University of Chicago Press, 1995). Rabindranath was a tireless world traveler; it is quite astonishing that, given his health at this time, he found the energy to travel to the Himalayas.

Line 3: "Bowing, palms pressed" (*namaskār*). The Indian custom of greeting by pressing both palms together, chest high. The practice is also commonplace in some parts of Southeast Asia, such as in Thailand and Cambodia. Although bowing is not necessary, one usually bows while doing *namaskār* to an older person. Given Rabindranath's age in 1940 and the veneration in which he was held, he was very likely greeted with bows.

On My Birthday 11

Line 13: "rhythms" (*mridanga*). *Mridanga* is a percussion instrument widely used in performances of South Indian classical music known as *Cārnātic* music. Whereas *tabla,* an important percussion instrument in *Hindusthāni* music (North Indian classical music), is well known outside India, *mridanga* is not as well known, thus the use of the "percussive" image of "rhythms" instead.

On My Birthday 14

This poem was written in Kalimpong, another eastern Himalayan hill station near Mongpu. Lines 8 and 17 are questions directed to Kalimpong.

Line 13: "in unplayed tunes" (*anāhata sure*). Indian philosophy of music conceives of an absolute musical note that has no material cause. The primordial transcendent sound, "om," which is the sonic equivalent of *Brahman,* is an example. This sound is *anāhata,* which in musical theory has a cosmic, sacred significance. "Unstruck" or "unplayed," which is used here, are close translations of *anāhata*—the note that sounds without being struck or played. *Sure* means "in tune" or "in melody."

On My Birthday 21

Rabindranath repeatedly sounded warnings about the dire consequences of nationalism. The best source for his views on nationalism is a collection of three lectures given in Japan and the United States called *Nationalism* (New Delhi: Macmillan, 1976). This poem was written a few days before the fall of Paris in June 1940.

Line 31: "Chinnamasta." Chinnamasta is one of the forms of Kali, the goddess of destruction and an important icon in Bengal. The image of this deity of cosmic destruction, severed head held in her hands, adds immeasurably to the dark tone of this poem. (The compound word *chinnamastā* signifies a severed head.)

On My Birthday 24

This is the earliest poem in the present collection. It is also the only poem in *On My Birthday* written in 1939 (the rest were done in 1940 and 1941).

Rabindranath was an active painter during the last fifteen years or so of his life. He painted regularly, health permitting, during the period when these final poems were written.

On My Birthday 27

Line 14: "Immersion" (*abagāhan-snān*). A literal translation would be "immersion-bath." The image evokes the Hindu custom of sacred bathing in the Ganges, in which the entire body is immersed in the river.

FROM *Last Poems*

Last Poems 2

Line 1: "Death-eclipse, that demon" (*rāhur matan mrityu*). A literal translation would be "Rahu-like death." Rahu is a demon believed to cause eclipses.

Last Poems 4

It is possible that the chair of this poem is the one that Rabindranath used in Argentina when he was a guest of Victoria Ocampo's, the famous editor of the influential *Sur* magazine. Rabindranath received the chair as a gift from Ocampo and brought it back to Shantiniketan. For an excellent account of their friendship, see Ketaki Kushari Dyson, *In Your Blossoming Flower-Garden: Rabindranath Tagore and Victoria Ocampo* (Dehli: Sahitya Akademi, 1988).

Line 6: "weeping" (*hāhākār*). *Hāhākār* refers, more precisely, to the *sound* of anguished, grief-stricken weeping.

Last Poems 13

This is perhaps the most famous of Rabindranath's later poems for the Bengali reader. In it, Rabindranath, the poet of modern India, echoes the silence of the first great poem of ancient Indian literature, the "Creation Hymn" ("Nāsadīya") of the Rig Veda (ca. 2000 BCE), in which the unanswerable question of Being was first asked. The "Creation Hymn" begins with the unforgettable line, "there was neither non-existence nor existence then." It ends with these remarkable lines:

> Who really knows? Who will here proclaim it? Whence
> was it produced? Whence is this creation? The gods
> came afterwards, with the creation of this universe. Who
> then knows whence it has arisen?

> Whence this creation has arisen—perhaps it formed itself,
> or perhaps it did not—the one who looks down on it, in
> the highest heaven, only he knows—or perhaps he does
> not know.
> (The Rig Veda, trans. Wendy Doniger O'Flaherty
> [Harmondsworth: Penguin Books, 1981]).

A whole tradition of sacred literature nurtures the phrase that each stanza of Rabindranath's poem ends with: "There was no answer."

Last Poems 14

Line 11: "cinema" (*chalacchabi*). Although the Bengali language usually reserves *chalachitra* for "cinema," both terms mean "moving picture." Rabindranath had an interest in cinema; at his request, Sergey Eisenstein's *Potemkin* (1925) was screened during his visit to the Soviet Union. Also interesting to note, the film version of Rabindranath's novel *Gora* (published in 1910; the film appeared in 1938) opens with a book being presented to him and, as he flips through it, the camera zooms in and we see the credits of the movie written on the pages.

—SARANINDRANATH TAGORE